Gentle Voice

By Tanya Crowley

Do you know my Father in heaven?

I call Him Papa.

He's so very BIG, but so close
I can hear Him whisper.

That's my most FAVOURITE thing to hear.

Yesterday Jacob was crying. Oliver took his favourite colour.

That wasn't fair, so I said "Oliver please give Jacob's crayon back"

... then I heard Papa's gentle, quiet voice say "I love you so, so much ...

... Look how brave you are"

So many times I want a friend to talk to.

It's nice to have someone next to me.

Last night I wanted to know all about the night sky.

But it was "No More Talking" time.

... then I heard Papa's gentle, quiet voice say
"I love you so, so much ...

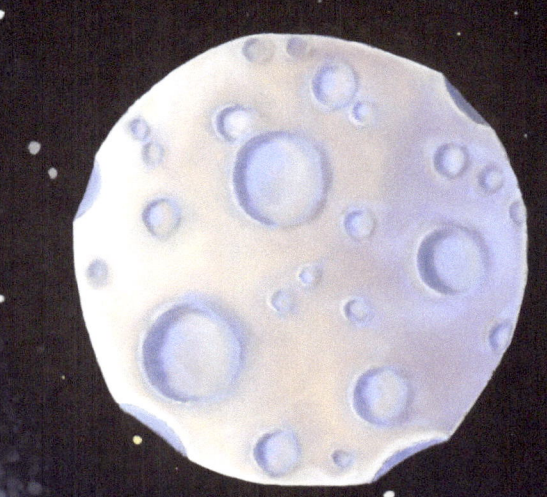

... Let me show you
what I've made"

I didn't like what I looked like in my reflection.

... then I heard Papa's gentle, quiet voice say "I love you so, so much ...

... Look how wonderfully I made you"

I was very, VERY angry.
I just wanted to SCREAM at my sister.

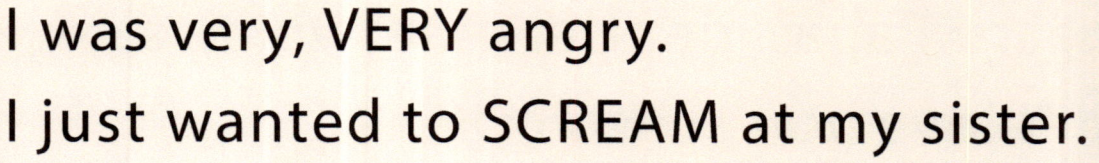

... then I heard Papa's gentle, quiet voice say
"I love you so, so much ...

...Let me help you find your words"

Sometimes I'm HAPPY ...

and sometimes SAD.

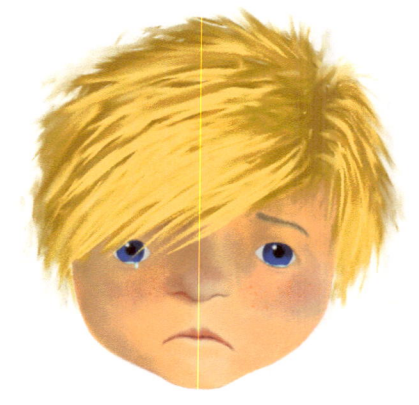

I can get very SILLY ...

and even a little bit MAD.

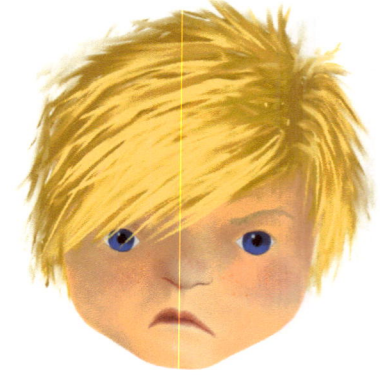

Papa doesn't mind.
He loves me EVERY way!

He knows me really well, and He still loves me.

When I was sitting on my own and everyone was busy, I thought no-one cared.

... then I heard Papa's gentle, quiet voice say
"I love you so, so much ...

... Tell me all about your day"

The other day I told my brother a joke.
It was the funniest I'd ever heard.

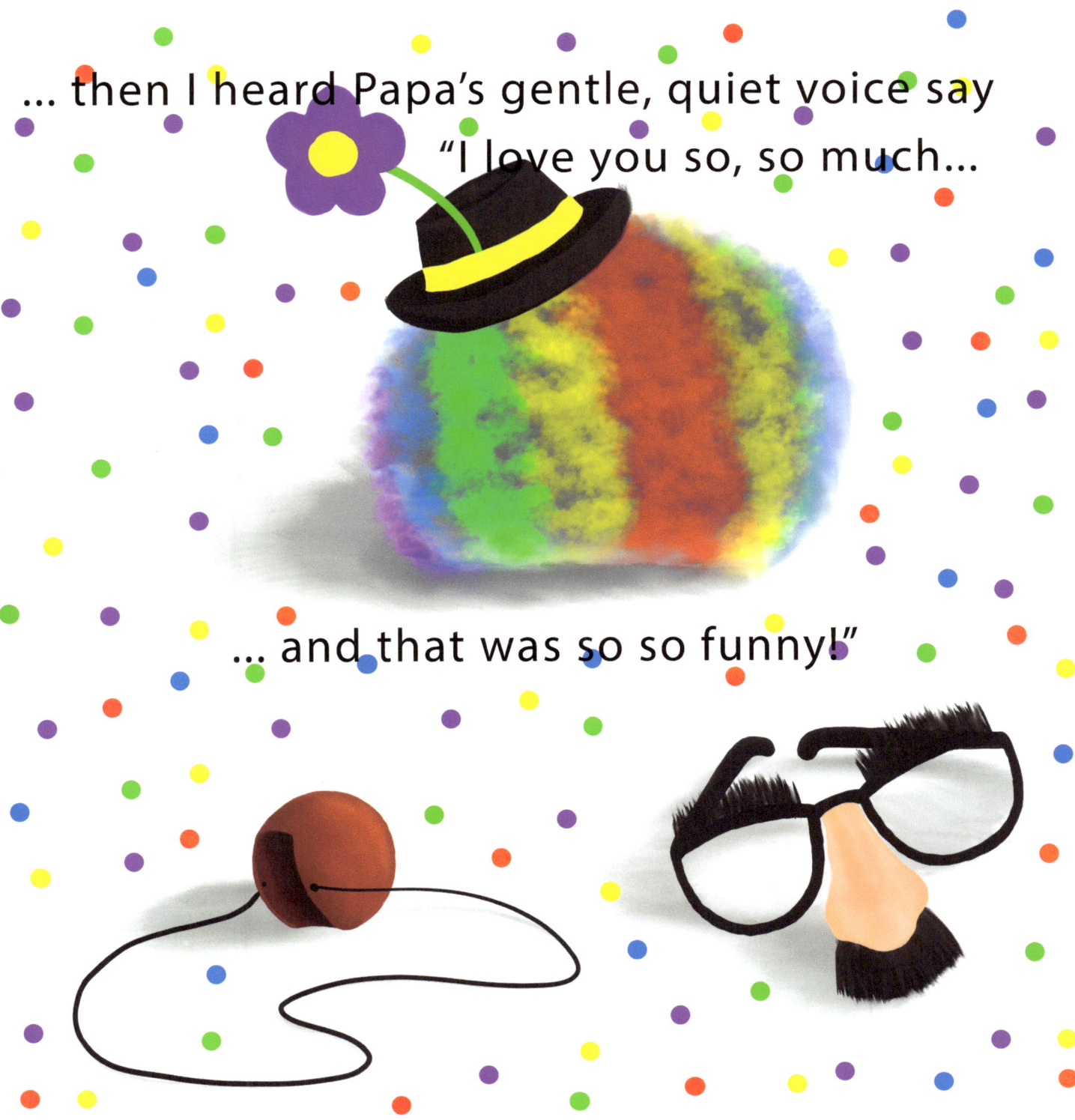

All night I kept seeing scary shadows.

I hid under my covers.

... then I heard Papa's gentle, quiet voice say
"I love you so, so much ...

... Let me hold you till morning"

I was talking to Mia the other day.
I told her all about my Papa in heaven.

But she already knows Papa just like me.
She told me how much He loves her.

My sister can do EVERYTHING way better.

I said I'd never EVER be as good.

... then I heard Papa's gentle, quiet voice say
"I love you so, so much ...

... You'll always be enough for me"

Today I was singing to my Papa.

I was pretty sure He liked my song.

... then I heard Papa's gentle, quiet voice say
"I love you so, so much ...

... I could listen to you sing all day"

It's nearly my birthday, but Bubbles said "I can't wait that long".

... then I heard Papa's gentle, quiet voice say "I love you so, so much ...

... Let's wait with Bubbles together"

Today I was thinking about YOU.

... then I heard Papa's gentle, quiet voice say "I love you so, so much ...

And, oh how much I love your new friend too"

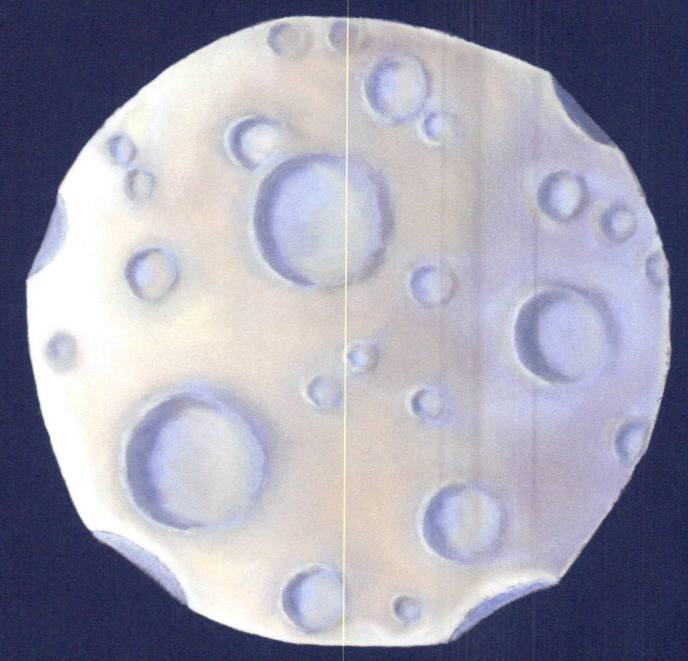

Published in Australia
by Tanya Crowley

© Text, Digital Illustrations and Cover Design
by Tanya Crowley, 2025
tcrowleybooks@gmail.com

Cataloguing-in-Publication data is available from
the National Library of Australia.

ISBN 978-0-6454836-3-5

www.ingramcontent.com/pod-product-compliance
Lightning Source LLC
Chambersburg PA
CBHW041203290426
44109CB00003B/111